SAVING AMERICA

Title: Saving America

ISBN-13: 978-1-942825-26-5

Author: Kambiz Mostofizadeh

Publisher: Mikazuki Publishing House

Copyright: 2019. All Rights Reserved.

Description: Saving America is a manifesto of American conservative thought which takes an in-depth look at the economic and problems facing America.

SAVING AMERICA

TABLE OF CONTENTS

SAVING AMERICA

Introduction

Americans have become more patriotic and more nationalistic since the election of Republican Donald Trump to the Presidency of the United States in 2016. Trump was just the tip of the iceberg, but his ascendance to the Presidency of the United States revealed a deep seated emergence of Americana. It was cool to love America again. Conservatism was the new counter-culture and it was influenced by such controversial figures such as Alex Jones. The love for America came back again in popular culture and tens of millions of Americans openly displayed American flags and American symbols to show their patriotism. This book is a Conservative manifesto of Conservative ideas on how to save America from the many economic and political problems it is facing. You as the reader should understand what Conservative ideology is about so that you can better understand what is being discussed. What is known as Conservative thought relies on a few principles that define its being. It is important to note that American Conservative ideology is unique to the United States of America and is different than for example a Conservative in Germany, France, or Australia.

SAVING AMERICA

Great To Be Poor

It seems like the media is filled with messages on how great it is to be poor. Everywhere they are talking about tiny homes and the tiny homes industry. After the loan debacle of 2007-2008 that sent global markets in to a recession, nearly 2 million Americans became homeless while Wall Street bankers were bailed out to the expense of the working and middle classes. Cities like Los Angeles and New York that were known for their affluence became centers of homelessness and poverty. California which is traditionally a Democratic state, has seen rising homelessness and crime. A city or municipality is a finite space with its own inhabitants and its own cultural nuances. When you open the floodgates and fail to prevent illegal immigration, you get cities like Los Angeles filled with people that are apathetic about their surroundings, because they had no participation in the creation of that environment. The mainstream media painted anyone that wanted legal immigration as being against immigration all together. There are only a finite number of jobs in a given area. When more people enter in to an area, legally or illegally, that takes away opportunities from people that inhabited the area originally. It would be like a village raiding another village in order to get their crops. There are only a limited amount of crops to be had. Socialism

SAVING AMERICA

is a scam because it wants you to
work hard and share your crops with
someone else. The only problem is
that the person you may be sharing
with may not be working at all or may
be working less than you. If you had
to share what you produced with
others then there would be no
incentive for you to work at all. Your
efforts would be wasted because
they would not be 100 percent yours.
This argument applies to taxes as
well. If I am going to give away 5
months of my earnings and keep 7
months, then there is no point in
working. We are all equal under the
law but we are not all equal in reality.
My neighbor drives a Porsche and I
don't. He went to Medical School
and spent 16 years of his life

SAVING AMERICA

studying Medicine. He makes more than me and he should, he deserves too. He spent his life studying medicine and I spent my life writing and hiking up hilltops. We are both equal under the law but we are not both equal financially and we don't deserve to be. I didn't spend my time in Medical School so why should I be angry that the person that did makes more than me? He has no obligation to share his salary with me just as I have no obligation to share my lunch with him. Our homes are not equal and how much we spend is not equal. Nothing that I have in common with my neighbor is equal, other than we are both males, and still that is not equal because my neighbor is taller and better looking

SAVING AMERICA

than me. Our equality is derived from the law that judges us both equally but fate will most certainly not deliver us an equal destiny. The only thing that we have in common is that we will both be punished, more or less, equally if we break the law. One judge might be more lenient and another judge harsher, but we will for the most part be judged equally under the law. Only under the law we are equal but in reality my neighbor has more than me. Should my neighbor be forced, under the law, to share half of his earnings from his labor with me? Should I be forced to share my earnings from my book sales with my neighbor? No. My neighbor did not spend thousands of hours writing in a room alone while

SAVING AMERICA

everyone was out having a great time. Nor did I spend thousands of hours on Medicine and studying the details of the human body. I don't deserve to share in the earnings of my neighbor and my neighbor doesn't get to share my earnings. Both of us should only keep what we made. Governments are there to provide services and to prevent wasteful practices. Governments are centers for the allocation of wealth and politics is the means and ways in which stakeholders allocate that wealth. When 7 Trillion Dollars is spent of wasteful military adventurism overseas, the domestic state suffers. The quality of life of Americans lowers. China, Russia, Japan, France, Netherlands, and

SAVING AMERICA

many other nations have High Speed
Rail Networks that connect them to
many nations allowing fast and
efficient travel. In America, there is
no High Speed Rail Network.
Everywhere on earth, nations are
investing massive amounts of money
in to infrastructure and development.
Building and maintaining an empire
is both expensive and time intensive.
The larger the governmental
bureaucracy grows, the more
domestic America suffers because of
it. The U.S. Government already
employs more than 2 million people,
making it the largest corporation on
earth. Over 20 Trillion Dollars in Debt
piled up with no end in sight because
politicians in DC rarely talk about it.
When the President of the United

SAVING AMERICA

States is unable to control fiscal and monetary policy this has real effects on the economy. Any effort by the U.S. President to reduce the gigantic governmental bureaucracy would result in the mainstream media portraying them in a negative light. The United States domestic infrastructure is starving for funding that is diverted elsewhere. 5000 bridges in need of serious repair and maintenance to prevent their collapse are bypassed in favor of foreign aid. Foreign Alliances with huge financial incentives are given more credence than domestic infrastructure. Nations are passing the United States in things like transportation, science, education, and manufacturing because they are

SAVING AMERICA

actively re-investing in those industries. The United States highly regulates all industries and creates so much red tape for new companies seeking to enter its markets that companies shy away after learning how difficult it is. The US could create Free Trade Zones that provide financial incentives to manufacturers that manufacture there. The US could lower its corporate tax rates further to compete with tax haven like areas like Hong Kong and Kuala Lumpur. Despite what naysayers believe, reducing taxes creates opportunities for business owners and corporations to spend more on things like equipment and hiring new personnel. The US has been called

SAVING AMERICA

at times a huge corporation and it would not be far from the truth. The Business of America is Business. The US has since the 1970's had a Corporatism style model with an economic partnership between the public and private sector. The 2008 Wall Street Bail Outs by the Obama Administration were further proof of this alliance. Conservatism wants small government and low bureaucracy but establishment Conservatives have done just the opposite, growing the National Debt by Trillions. George Bush Sr and Jr were both Conservatives. Both of them grew the Debt by Trillions due to their Military Adventurism. All of this spending without re-investment in civil infrastructure has created an

SAVING AMERICA

America starving for progress in the face of nations around the globe that are building massive civil infrastructure projects like Bridges, Roadways, and High Speed Trains. The Corporatism of the New Right has sold out the Middle Class in favor of factories built in Mexico and China. Globalization is also known as Americanization, because the values of America are sent overseas alongside the products they are selling. For example, the person sipping a Coca-Cola is really accessing America and feeling American by drinking it. Globalization lead to horrible deals like NAFTA that crippled U.S. businesses making them regulated by an international agreement they never wanted. The

SAVING AMERICA

United States has invested in
technology companies internally
since the 1950's with the purpose of
having an advantage over the Soviet
Union during the Cold War. This
spread in to the movie industry and
Hollywood with branches of the U.S.
Military meeting with and providing
assistance to movie production
companies. Jerry Bruckheimer
movies like Top Gun featuring Tom
Cruise could only be made because
they received massive amounts of
assistance from the U.S. Navy.
Aircraft, aircraft carriers, and Navy
personnel were featured in the movie
Top Gun. What would it cost for a
movie production to rent out an
Aircraft Carrier? It would cost you
nothing if your movie would present

SAVING AMERICA

the U.S. Navy, for example, in a positive light. Movie production companies rely on this type of assistance as it provides a huge funding boon for them and saves them millions of dollars. As long as the movie is supportive and positive towards the U.S. Military, the movie producer becomes open to receiving potentially tens of millions of dollars in assistance. A lot of movies are viewed as being pure American advertising and that is because they are. The U.S. Government has a deep alliance with Hollywood as well as with Silicon Valley (the center of American innovation and technology). This alliance has allowed for the propagation of American values through American

SAVING AMERICA

movies. It started during the Cold War as a means to counter the Soviet Union but continued in Hollywood as a means to call out whoever was the foe of the day. This propagation caused people from around the world to want to flee to America. It caused them to want to have the lives of the people on Dallas, Dynasty, Friends, Desperate Housewives, and 24. Except those are TV shows and are fictional whereas life is real and does not resemble a television show. Channels like MTV, which created the Music Video, promoted American ideals of liberalism overseas. You can go to almost any nation on earth and see a Teenager wearing a Metallica T-shirt. American values

SAVING AMERICA

were purposefully packaged and sold through popular culture, whether or not the popular culture was demeaning or offensive. The idea that you could be free and demeaning was celebrated as an American value. Kim Kardashian was posing her butt as naked on magazine covers and this was sold as American as apple pie by the Liberal heads of media companies. As if lacking in public morality, makes you better than others because that somehow denotes you are free. The system pushes Globalization or Americanization because it benefits by promoting American Global Leadership. Many of these values are just Liberalism packaged for public consumption but they contribute to bringing the worst elements of the world to the United States because they believed the messages spread to them by the musical, literary, and movie products they consumed. It has been a strategy of the Hollywood Military Industrial Complex to do this and it has been done deliberately to convince the world of American supremacy.

2ND Amendment

The United States Constitution clearly states that Americans have the right to bear arms. This means that they have the right to purchase things like rifles or handguns. The United States Army which started in 1775 started with arms (rifles). The

SAVING AMERICA

militias of the original 13 Colonies
(New Hampshire, Massachusetts,
Rhode Island, Connecticut, New
York, New Jersey, Pennsylvania,
Delaware, Maryland, Virginia, North
Carolina, South Carolina, Georgia)
were armed. The militias in modern
America are armed. It is the right of
Americans to purchase arms and to
bear arms. No protest or body can
take away this right from Americans.
The rise of mass shootings in
America has created panic among
Liberals who want to take away the
Right to Bear Arms for Americans.
Politicians like Beto O'Rourke have
promised to take away guns from
Americans all together through a
buy-back program. Some Americans
do hunt but it is important to note

SAVING AMERICA

that the reason Americans have gun
is not for duck hunting. Americans
cherish their Right to Bear Arms
because it is a traditional form of
self-defense in the United States.
Thomas Jefferson viewed guns and
rifles as a means of self defense
against tyranny and was heavily
involved with the Virginia Militia. The
Frontiersmen like Davy Crockett and
Jim Bowie slept with their rifles and
guns beside them. Rifles and guns
are an American tradition that has
existed since America's inception.
Rifles and guns have played a
critical role in the conquest of North
America and the defense of the
United States in the Revolutionary
War, War of 1812, and Civil War. If
Americans did not have rifles and

SAVING AMERICA

guns there would be no United States of America. George Washington and the Founding Fathers believed that the 2nd Amendment protects the rest of the rights of Americans. In other words, they believed that without the Right To Bear Arms, all other rights would be at risk of being usurped by an Authoritarian style government. The colonists wanted things like:

- Freedom of expression
- Freedom of speech
- Freedom of assembly
- Freedom to petition the government
- Freedom of worship
- The right to bear arms

The Founding Fathers were already suspicious of England, their King, and his army of Redcoats. The Founding Fathers believed that rifles and guns were the only way to establish true freedom in the face of tyranny and tyrannical governments. As for mass shootings, only a small percentage of them have been carried out by people with machine guns and automatic weapons. The majority of mass shootings have been carried out by psychopaths with mental disabilities or mental problems brandishing handguns. Humans pull triggers, triggers do not pull themselves. Just because a few psychopaths out of 320 million people commit horrid acts does not mean that Americans should lose their Right To Bear Arms. Mass shootings and other such horrific acts are the works of criminals and psychopaths. 320 Million people do not lose their rights because a few psychopathic criminals decide to break the law. Women are beginning to attend gun ranges and to purchase guns in higher frequency to protect themselves against things like rape. Citizens armed could prevent things like public crime as has been proven countless times in nations like Brazil where off-duty cops and ordinary citizens are armed and watchful. If a foreign nation ever decided to invade the United States, the US Army would be the least of their worries. They would have to contend with a few hundred million Armed Americans defending their family and defending their homes.

SAVING AMERICA

Americans view the 2nd Amendment and the Right To Bear Arms as being Sacrosanct. It is a Sacred Right they view as coming from the U.S. Constitution and being endorsed by the Founding Fathers of the United States. The Constitution described how the new government would be organized, how government officials would be chosen, and what rights the new central government would guarantee to citizens. The members of the Constitutional Convention approved the Constitution on September 17, 1787. Next, all 13 states had to approve it. Some people felt that the Constitution did not do enough to protect the rights of individual people. The states agreed to approve the Constitution if a list of

SAVING AMERICA

individual rights were added to it.
The states approved the Constitution
in 1789. This list of individual rights,
called the Bill of Rights, was added
to the Constitution in 1791. Changes
to the Constitution are called
"amendments." The first 10
amendments to the Constitution are
called the Bill of Rights. If it were not
for the Right To Bear Arms,
frontiersman could never venture
West and occupy lands that would
be eventually joined as part of the
United States. The United States
was created by the gun, protected by
the gun, and preserved by the gun.
The gun allowed the new world
Americans to conquer North America
and to tame the Native American
tribes occupying it. The advances in

SAVING AMERICA

gun technology allowed American soldiers to finally compete with and defeat the warrior-like Native Americans. In early skirmishes with Native Americans, the Colonists would lose every time because the Native Americans would be able to shoot 10 Arrows by the time the Colonial was able to load and fire 1 Shot. The traditional Native American Bow and Arrow, despite being an ancient weapon, was vastly advanced in speed and range in comparison to the crude guns and rifles used by early American colonials. American colonials were hardly good shots and had weapons that were mostly inaccurately fired, whereas the Native Americans had spent many years practicing and

SAVING AMERICA

mastering the Bow. It was only with the development of gun and rifle technology that Americans were able to conquer the rest of North America and to establish routes. The road West was harsh and difficult, with American settlers having to pass through many Native American lands. The American colonials were under constant attack from Native Americans and guns and rifles were there only means of defense. In modern America, guns and rifles are the only defense Americans have against criminals. By the time the Police arrive, the people that called the Police might be dead or badly injured. In some cases, the Police might not arrive at all or arrive very late, making self-defense the only option available. The Police or Law Enforcement Official will not always be available to you. Defending yourself and your family may be the only option that you can choose. In most cases, the home intruder or criminal looking to harm you will be armed and dangerous.

Pizzagate

A hoax spread through social media regarding a pizza parlor engaged in human trafficking and pedophilia. What is a reality is that, according to FBI numbers, 900,000 children go missing every year in the United States of America. They are either kidnapped or lost. Where on earth could nearly 1 million humans a year go missing and no one notice? If this

SAVING AMERICA

happened in any developed or undeveloped nation on earth, it would be the object of mainstream media. Why is the American mainstream media so silent on this matter? The CPS of Child Protective Services should turn its focus to these 900,000 children that go missing every year in America. Human trafficking is a global epidemic and a multi-billion dollar business. Many of the 900,000 children that go missing every year are found but what about the American children that go missing and are never heard from or seen again? Who is searching for them? Loved ones, but they can only search for so long before giving up the endeavor. Why has the Federal

SAVING AMERICA

Government turned their focus to these hundreds of thousands of missing children? Most of the children that are kidnapped are taken by a family member, whether distant or close. The Right taunted one Conspiracy Theory about a pizza parlor and the Left went wild with rage without ever even once mentioning the 900,000 children that go missing every year in America. Where was the collective outrage for the missing? The Left was silent just as they were when President Barack Hussein Obama created 50 Million Refugees in the Middle East and North Africa by invading Iraq, Libya, Syria, and Afghanistan. The Left should not be angry about a Conspiracy Theory. The Left should

SAVING AMERICA

be angry that 900,000 children go
missing but instead they deflect by
acting shocked over a pizza parlor
conspiracy. Human trafficking affects
American commerce, American
quality of life, and American culture
just as much as any other. Crime
and criminal elements bring
criminality in to a culture they are
criminally operating in. America is no
exception. Criminals traffic humans
from Mexico in to the United States.
According to some reports, up to 85
percent of all women that are
crossing the Mexico-United States
border illegally are raped before they
reach the United States. 85 percent.
Many of these Women go missing
when they reach the United States
because their family members in

SAVING AMERICA

Mexico are unable to pay the "Ransom Release Fee". If the Ransom Release Fee is not paid by a family member of the person being illegally smuggled in to the United States, then that person is held as a Hostage to be used for Sexual Slavery. The people fleeing from the war-zone like Mexican crime back home are exploited by the very people that are pretending to help them.

Affirmative Action
Minorities like Blacks and Mexicans are given priority to be hired for a job because Whites will. Affirmative Action, as a designated government policy, has made White Americans poorer and has made them suffer

economically. Minorities like Blacks and Mexicans are given to priority to enter universities and colleges while Whites with higher test scores are left behind because "there wasn't enough space in the program". I was personally denied entry in to multiple Masters Programs in Political Science in California because "there wasn't enough space in the program". Why do you think this was? It is because Blacks and Mexicans were given preferential treatment to get in the program while students like me that graduated Magna Cum Laude where denied and turned away. Affirmative Action hurts the United States by not adhering to a Merit Based educational system. The Merit Based

SAVING AMERICA

jobs system is hurt equally when top candidates are brushed off in favor of lower ranked candidates that happen to be a minority. The candidate with the better resume and greater experience should be hired in every case but Affirmative Action has derailed that. In the education system, the student with the higher GPA, higher scores, and higher marks should be granted access to Higher Education and the student with lower GPA and lower test scores should be the one turned away. Using race to select students is not fair to students that studied harder and did better academic work. Affirmative Action is viewed by many as a form of Reverse Racism, where Whites are punished for

SAVING AMERICA

perceived historical wrongs and
Black and Mexicans are rewarded by
the system to correct the historical
wrongs. Why should Whites in
America have to suffer for what their
ancestors may or may not have
done? If that is the case then
everywhere should answer and be
held accountable for what someone
else has done. An illogical argument
but it is promoted as normal and
beneficial. Beneficial to whom? Why
should Whites, who are poor and
middle and upper class, suffer
because of what a few racist
misguided slave owners did 300
years ago? How is that just or
serving the purpose of justice?
Affirmative Action is a policy that has
stoked the fires of Racism and

NaN# SAVING AMERICA

contributed to creating racists in society. It is a policy that is out-dated and against the principles of a free Republic that promotes equality.

Build The Wall

Even to say "Build the Wall" was deemed as Racist and Xenophobic by the Mainstream Media and the Liberal establishment. Building a Border Wall on the southern border of the United States with Mexico, was started as a unifying chant for protecting America from illegal immigrants. There are many immigrants (like myself) that had to spend hundreds of thousands of dollars in costs to get a U.S. Citizenship. Hundreds of thousands of dollars? Yes. Hundreds of

SAVING AMERICA

thousands of dollars flying back and forth, paying for hotels, paying for apartments, paying for cars, paying for routine bills, and paying for the normal expenses that a human incurs. Why should someone get to sneak in for free? Why should people get to get for free what I spent hundreds of thousands to get? Americans are not against immigration, but we are against illegal immigration. Nations have laws that have to be followed because the law applies equally to all, whether legal or illegal immigrant. Countless American tourists have been murdered in Mexico for no other reason than they were a fish out of water. In other words, they didn't look like a local so a local took

SAVING AMERICA

advantage of them by robbing and murdering them. It is not just Americans that are at risk in Mexico, but Mexicans themselves face serious risks. Drug Gangs control large areas and Mexican Police are corrupt. If the Police don't extort money from you and falsely put you in prison in order to get paid, you stand the chance of being kidnapped and murdered by a Drug Gang. Heads are decapitated and bodies are buried in the desert. Dangerous would not be an adequate word to describe life in Mexico for Mexicans and for foreigners. Building the Wall would benefit the United States because Open Borders cost the US Billions of Dollars a Year. If an effective Border Wall prevented

SAVING AMERICA

illegal immigrants from entering the
United States, then billions of dollars
a year could be saved on Border
Patrol Agents. Tens of billions of
dollars are spent on manpower to
guard a nearly un-guardable border
that lacks a wall. A proper Border
Wall would not need 30,000 Border
Patrol Agents. A proper Border Wall
would need 500 Border Patrol
Agents. The reason why there are so
many Border Patrol Agents is
because there isn't a Border Wall. A
Border Wall would prevent the flow
of dangerous drugs in to the United
States and it would stop the flow of
human trafficking over the Southern
Border. Human Traffickers are not
only engaged in one type of
criminality, they are involved in

several forms of criminality. Women
that are trafficked from Mexico in to
the United States, are many times
forced to carry drugs and contraband
with them as a form of travel
payment. Videos have been
released publicly showing bales of
drugs being carried by illegal
immigrants followed by armed
handlers watching over them. Mad
Max style cars outfitted like tanks
with weapons of war carry illegal
immigrants and drugs to the United
States border. Lawlessness at its
best and criminality at its worst.
Many of the cities and towns in the
United States complain about the
influx of drugs and illegal immigrants
causing crime in their cities.
Caravans of illegal immigrants

SAVING AMERICA

disrupt life not only for Americans but also for those nations which they are passing through, like Mexico. Central American illegal immigrants from various nations put a strain and burden on Mexican civil services as much as American civil services. Immigration is acceptable and part of American culture when it is done legally. Illegal Immigration puts pressure on local governments and create inequality in society. Minorities like African-Americans or Black Americans put illegal immigration as one of the problems facing them because the influx of illegal immigrants has caused racial tension in their own community. In Los Angeles, there have been numerous incidents of violence

SAVING AMERICA

between Mexicans and Blacks over
areas to live in. Blacks view illegal
immigration as taking away from
their own rights. There have been
numerous incidents of violence by
illegal immigrants against White
Americans as well. There have been
many illegal immigrants that
achieved legal status and are
upstanding and noble members of
American society. Nations around
the world have a Merit Based
Immigration System where they
grant legal immigrant status to
educated and industrious individuals
like Doctors, Lawyers, Engineers,
Scientists, Athletes, and other skilled
individuals. In other words, nations
with Merit Based Immigration
Systems only want the best and

SAVING AMERICA

brightest coming to their country.
Everyone is welcome to apply but
only the best are granted legal
immigrant status. The cream of the
crop is sought after and that is what
makes certain nations like Australia
thrive. In nations like Australia and
Canada, Merit Based Immigration
has worked successfully and allowed
their nations to prosper by only
bringing in individuals that will benefit
society as well as benefitting
themselves. It is not racist to want
Merit Based Legal Immigration. It is
criminal to demand that individuals
that broke the law should be given
preferential treatment in spite of it.
The United States is a nation of laws
and those want to enter the United
States should do so legally. Illegal

SAVING AMERICA

Immigrants can be great or they can be horrible. It is a coin toss. If a Merit Based Immigration System is put in place, the applicants will have been previously vetted and handpicked based on their skillsets and education. The best and the brightest should be brought in, not the worst the earth has to offer. A ship may have a capacity of 100 and the inhabitants of that ship are asking for 500 people to get on. The ship ends up sinking. Everything has a capacity. This is not to say that the capacity of the United States is 320 Million. The capacity of the United States may be 3 Billion, but can the economy sustain 3 Billion? Can the environment sustain 3 Billion? Can government services sustain 3

SAVING AMERICA

Billion? The more people there are,
the lower of quality of life you will
have because money and resources
are finite. The United States should
handpick the amount of people that
can enter and instead of creating
quotas for each nation it should
create ceilings or limits for each
nation. Regardless of if limits are set
for nations or not, the system should
be a Merit Based System that favors
the smartest and most skilled
individuals that could provide a
benefit to society. The main reasons
that people immigrate to America are
the following:

- Freedom
- Political liberty
- Religious freedom
- Economic opportunity

SAVING AMERICA

- Escape persecution

The Liberals love illegal immigration
because it allows them to play the
virtue signaling Social Justice
Warrior, when in fact they care
nothing about it as proven when they
remained silent when President
Barack Hussein Obama deported 2
million people during his 8 years in
office. Building the Wall is seen as
horrific by the Liberals when the
Liberals themselves have huge walls
around their own homes. Liberals
live in suburban gated communities
but don't want to gate off the border
preventing the flow of drugs and
crime? Why do you lock your doors
before you sleep? To prevent an
intruder from entering your home. A

SAVING AMERICA

Border Wall prevents intruders from bringing drugs and contraband with them to the US. A Border Wall prevents criminals from bringing crime and dangerous criminals with them to the US. A Border Wall makes America safer.

Death To Murderers

If you murder another human being, then the State should try you and if you are convicted of murder, then you should be murdered by the State. Capital Punishment should be mandatory for Murderers, if they are proven to be guilty of Murder beyond a shadow of a doubt. Criminals are treated too lightly and it has emboldened criminals. The Left loves to talk about how bad the

SAVING AMERICA

Police are and about Police Brutality, but will call the Police to protect them at the first sight of trouble. Ironic isn't it? Criminals that are out to harm you could care less if you have called the Police or not, they will continue to carry out the crime unless you are armed and able to protect yourself and your family. By the time the Police arrive it could be too late. The Police should be funded adequately so that they can provide their services to citizens in a timely manner. If Police are under-manned then they will not be able to provide their services to citizenry in a timely and even manner. Either the Police have to protect you (which they will not be able to do because they are not always there) or you have to

SAVING AMERICA

protect yourself and your family. If someone is coming to murder you and they are successful, then they should be tried for Murder, and if found Guilty, they should be executed (murdered) legally by the State. If a human takes a human life and get 4 years in jail, what message does that send to criminals? That they will barely receive a slap on the wrist if they commit murder. It will not only not discourage them but it may embolden them. If Murderers are executed then that will send the message to Murderers that crimes like Murder will receive the sentence of Capital Punishment. Capital Punishment is the only true deterrent to criminals that intend to murder human beings.

SAVING AMERICA

De-Regulation

Over-regulation has created an environment in America that stifles business. Bureaucracy and red-tape prevent businesses from starting and they prevent businesses from innovating. Free market capitalism should be the order of the day but the bureaucrats which run the U.S. pull the economic strings of businesses by telling them what they can and can't do. The bureaucrats decide which businesses can merge and which businesses can be sold to other businesses. Businesses are forced to re-locate because they cannot compete on a global scale with nations like China. I personally know of at least one company in Los Angeles, California that manufactured coat hangers. Not a complex product but still one that relies on machinery and manpower to see it through. The last time I drove past this company, all I saw were boarded up windows and locked doors. The coat hanger company had moved to China because it could not compete with cheap Chinese coat hangers that had been dumped on to the U.S. market for a few pennies a piece. The Chinese are not to blame in this case, rather it is the un-business like policies that regulated this American coat hanger manufacturer in to bankruptcy that should be blamed. The greater the regulation on business the less productivity will ensue causing businesses to have to

SAVING AMERICA

close their operations in the U.S. and move to Mexico, China, and other cheap manufacturing hubs. Free market capitalism relies on the free market to meet the demands of consumers and the interference of the government through crippling policies has stifled business creation and business innovation. Governmental interference is detrimental because it prevents businesses from making the best decision for themselves. The "best decision" is dictated to them and businesses are forced to follow the guidelines or face citations. Saving America will depend on the de-regulation of markets and the absence of interference in the affairs of businesses and corporations.

SAVING AMERICA

Foreign Alliances

Establishment Conservatives have become Globalist Neo-Conservatives that favor and root for Military Adventurism, Empire Building, and global Hegemony. The Founding Fathers were not for foreign wars. The Founding Fathers were about Isolationism. The United States has spent the last 224 out of the past 241 years in wars such as:

- War of 1812
- Mexican-American War
- Civil War
- Spanish-American War
- World War I
- World War II
- Korean War
- Vietnam War
- (Persian) Gulf War

SAVING AMERICA

The policy of the Founding Fathers
was that if it is not happening on
American soil, then it does not
concern the United States of
America. George Washington
warned the United States about
Foreign Alliances in his Farewell
Address by saying "Why quit our
own to stand upon foreign ground?
Why, by interweaving our destiny
with that of any part of Europe,
entangle our peace and prosperity in
the toils of European ambition,
rivalry, interest, humor or caprice?
It is our true policy to steer clear of
permanent alliances with any portion
of the foreign world; so far, I mean,
as we are now at liberty to do it; for
let me not be understood as capable
of patronizing infidelity to existing

engagements. I hold the maxim no less applicable to public than to private affairs, that honesty is always the best policy. I repeat it, therefore, let those engagements be observed in their genuine sense. But, in my opinion, it is unnecessary and would be unwise to extend them." George Washington, the 1st President of the United States and Founding Father, clearly warned against the United States entangling itself in foreign alliances. The modern United States has become a web of foreign entanglements from the United States' relationship with Israel to the United States' relationship with Saudi Arabia. These foreign alliances have not only created international pressure on the United

SAVING AMERICA

States but have also fueled domestic conspiracy theories and domestic opposition to these alliances. 72 Percent of the United States is White and Christian and they view foreign alliances with Israel and Saudi Arabia as being against the wishes and beliefs of the Founding Fathers of the United States. Israel and its virtual control over the U.S. Congress have allowed for the creation of such conspiracy theories. Conspiracy theories may be 90 percent false but they still rest on 10 percent of truth. Israel and Saudi Arabia have taken the lead in lobbying and making payments to members of the U.S. Congress. It is legal in the United States and nations like Saudi Arabia and Israel have taken full advantage by nearly paying every member of Congress through lobbyists. Pay For Play has become the standard in Washington DC and the nations lining up to make payments through a Lobbyist in order to influence the outcome of a vote are many. If Americans have lost faith in their system it is because they see the system as being either in gridlock or bought and paid for by corporations and/or foreign governments. Much of the current Military Adventurism of the United States is bought and paid for by nations like South Korea, Saudi Arabia, Israel, and others that are unable to adequately protect themselves from military threats. The payments may not be direct but they

SAVING AMERICA

come in the form of huge trade deals. Foreign Alliances are dangerous and tricky to manage. The United States has to support South Korea out of fear of North Korea, potentially putting the United States on a collision course to go to War with China. Overseas military bases are outposts of the Pax Americana (American Empire) that protect Foreign Allies from military threat. The current United States presence in Poland is to deter Russia. The Cold War continuing 30 years later and still going strong. The United States pays over 30 Billion Dollars a year to Israel and 1 Billion Dollars a year to Egypt so that they don't fight each and act like friends. US Taxpayer Dollars are wasted on

SAVING AMERICA

fruitless overseas endeavors. The United States has spent nearly 20 years fighting a War on Terrorism that has had seen the United States spend 7 Trillion Dollars. Was this War fought on behalf of the American people? Why was Iraq invaded when 15 of the 19 hijackers in 9/11 were from Saudi Arabia? The interests of the American people is in defense of America. The U.S. Army is not For Rent and at the beck and call of foreign nations. An Isolationist Approach is what will save America. Money given to Foreign Nations should cease and all the Tens of Billions of Dollars should be spent on civil infrastructure and education. The U.S. is not responsible for the economic or political situation of

SAVING AMERICA

nations around the world. The U.S. should not play the Policeman of the World. The U.S. should focus on building the greatest nation on earth and that means bringing back its wealth for re-investment back home. Money spent overseas is wasted money. Americans needs that money in America and invested in the economy. How does giving 30 Billion to Israel and 1 Billion to Egypt and Billions of Dollars to other nations help the United States of America? If you have to pay someone to be your friend the chances are that they are not your friend. All of those billions of dollars will make a huge impact in the lives of Americans when they are brought back home. Tens of thousands of

SAVING AMERICA

new jobs will be created, the life will
be brought back to factories, and
new businesses will be created.
Every dollar sent overseas and not
spent domestically on Americans in
America is a dollar that is wasted.
Americans in America need the
money and the American economy
needs the money. Apple has recently
brought back over 1 Billion dollars in
profits back to America and is re-
investing it in America resulting in
the creation of thousands of jobs.
Making America Great Again
depends on the repatriation of funds
that were derived overseas.
American goods are sought out
throughout the world but American
companies, such as tech companies
like Facebook, Google, and even

SAVING AMERICA

Apple, have sought out foreign lands for incorporation in order to reduce their taxes in America. Money shouldn't be spend on foreign alliances or on tax breaks for corporations. Money should be spent on Americans and the money should be invested in civil infrastructure. Money given to Israel or to Saudi Arabia or to Burkina Faso or anywhere else only strengthens their nations and financially and morally weakens Americans back home. The vote for Donald Trump in the Presidential Election of 2016 was a referendum on the state of the nation. Americans had become tired of 8 years of foreign invasions and wasting precious time on a national healthcare plan that never materialized. Hillary Clinton, as Secretary of State, pushed the United States in to various military conflicts overseas and created a tense atmosphere between The White House and the U.S. military. Anyone that was declared an enemy of foreign alliances of the U.S. was declared an enemy to the U.S. effectively tangling the U.S. in foreign military adventurism. Obama deployed troops to Afghanistan like his predecessors. Afghanistan has traditionally been the graveyard of empires, as can be attested to by the British, Russians, and others. Foreign alliances pushed the United States in to Iraq, foreign alliances pushed the United States in to Afghanistan, foreign alliances

SAVING AMERICA

pushed the United States in to Syria, and foreign alliances pushed the United States in to Libya. Were the Afghan, Libyan, Syrian, or Iraqi armies invading or threatening the United States? No it is the Foreign Alliance with Saudi Arabia that pushed the United States in to Syria. It is the Foreign Alliance with Saudi Arabia and Israel that pushed the United States in to Iraq. It is the Foreign Alliance with Saudi Arabia that pushed the United States in to Afghanistan. It is the Foreign Alliance with Saudi Arabia that pushed the United States in to Afghanistan. Al-Qaeda, Taliban, Al-Shabab, ISIL, ISIS, Al Nusra Front, and other Sunni Wahabi terrorist organizations are directly controlled

SAVING AMERICA

and funded by Saudi Arabia. The
9/11 Commission established that 15
of the 19 hijackers came from Saudi
Arabia yet the United States still
chooses to sell 100 Billion Dollars'
worth of weapons to Saudi Arabia
despite the chance that some of
those weapons could end up in the
hands of Sunni Wahabi Islamists
(extremists). Saudi Arabia spends
tens of billions of dollars per year
funding *madrasas* or religious
schools that teach an extremist
version of Islam. The United States
has full knowledge that a large
portion of the money given to
Pakistan has found its way in to the
hands of Sunni Wahabi Islamists that
have used those same weapons to
carry out attacks on American

soldiers. The danger in giving nations money is that you are unable to control how that money will be used and in many times it has been used to carry out terrorist attacks. Foreign alliances are used in many instances to counter what could be perceived as a threat to the United States. Temporary Alliances or Alliances Based on Convenience can assist the United States without the U.S. having to make it permanent, thereby entangling America in the domestic affairs of other nations. Alliances based on things like fighting terrorism or carrying out humanitarian missions are beneficial to the United States, but only if there are measurable parameters that define failure and success. Foreign alliances can help the United States but for the most part they hinder and deny the sovereignty of the United States by causing it to become entangled in the problems of the allied nation. Why should the average American care what happens in Israel? Or Saudi Arabia? How that is relevant to the life of the working class American? How is that relevant to the life of the middle class American? Why should American soldiers risk their lives for Saudi Arabia when 15 of the 19 9/11 hijackers came from Saudi Arabia? What incentive is there for American soldiers to risk their lives for Saudi Arabia when it is public knowledge that Saudi Arabia is funding and

SAVING AMERICA

supporting terrorist groups? America should pursue isolationism and should shun foreign alliances. Foreign alliances put American soldiers at risk, foreign alliances deliver America in to situations that are un-warranted, and foreign alliances erode the political confidence that the American public have for political leaders. If members of the U.S. Congress receive payments from foreign nations, then how could it ever be believed that what they do is independent of foreign influence? If Foreign Governments are making payments to members of Congress it has to be automatically accepted that it is being done to influence those members of Congress. Money is not

SAVING AMERICA

paid for nothing, rather it is done because of an expectation of a political favor or to gain. What is to be gained? Political Favor, from arguably the most powerful Congressional Body on earth. There are reports that many members of Congress receive on average 1 million dollars per year from special interests like Israel and Saudi Arabia. As an added bonus, lavish trips with no expense spared, private jets, and luxury suites are provided for the chance to influence members of the U.S. Congress. The stakes are high and foreign nations like Israel and Saudi Arabia that benefit by receiving tens of billions of dollars in aid are among the most ardent lobbyists of Congress, cajoling and

SAVING AMERICA

persuading Congressional representatives to give them this or that advantage. The Alliance of the United States with Israel and Saudi Arabia is weighing down the United States and entangling it in the domestic affairs of those nations. The United States, arguably, had its greatest period during the 1920's and 1930's, incidentally when it was engaged wholeheartedly in isolationism. America's economy boomed and there was almost an electric like atmosphere of optimism that was publicly felt. America was heavily invested in America and the focus of America was America. World War II changed that. Europe was in ruins and England was badly hurt because of it. The only Western

SAVING AMERICA

democracy standing strong after
World War Two was the United
States. The massive investment in
infrastructure in the 1920's and
1930's had made the United States
the world leader in industry and
military by the 1940's (World War II).
Because the United States was the
only Western democracy standing
after World War Two, the United
States took on the role of the
policeman of the world. It was only
able to do this by strengthening the
alliances it currently had with France
and England. This entangled the
United States in the affairs, intrigues,
and plots of the French and English,
creating further military obligations
for the United States to police parts
of the empires that were part of

SAVING AMERICA

France and England. The creation of Israel, which lead to a rise in Anti-Semitism not before witnessed in American politics, was sanctioned by the United States and funded by American Jewish bankers like the Rothschild family. This added a further alliance that now entangled the United States in the affairs of the Middle East and North Africa. The many Israeli military conflicts with Egypt, Jordan, Syria, and Lebanon further entangled the United States in the affairs of Israel. The United States' dependence on oil, despite itself being the world's largest oil producer, spurred an alliance with the oil rich nation of Saudi Arabia. Saudi Aramco is a joint Saudi Arabian and American venture which

SAVING AMERICA

has given Saudi Arabia leverage over the internal and foreign politics of the United States. Saudi Arabia has enriched its rulers and used portions of oil proceeds to fund Terrorists like ISIS, ISIL, Taliban, Al-Qaeda, Al Nusra Front, and Al-Shabab. Everyone has full knowledge that 15 of the 19 hijackers behind 9/11 were from Saudi Arabia but no American politician dares speak out against Saudi Arabia for fear of being ostracized. U.S. Politicians think to themselves about the consequences of Saudi Arabia denying oil and gas to the United States, causing oil prices to rise and their constituents to vote them out of office. Foreign alliances entangle one nation to the

SAVING AMERICA

domestic and foreign policies of another nation, causing un-seen problems from such alliance. The Saudi Arabia is funding Terrorism but the United States can't stop them because if they do, the oil could stop flowing to America causing prices to double or triple overnight. This has created a horrible dilemma for American statesmen. Is it more important to fight the threat of Terrorism as funded by Saudi Arabia or is it more important to get cheap oil so my constituents will be happy? This is how the Foreign Alliance with Saudi Arabia has been able to get away with funding ISIS, ISIL, Al-Qaeda, Taliban, Al Nusra Front, Al-Shabab and others. American politicians in the U.S. Congress,

SAVING AMERICA

according to some reports, each
receive up to 1 Million Dollars per
year from Saudi Arabia. Why would
any of these Congresspersons have
any incentive to vote against Saudi
Arabia on anything? Their
constituents are far away from D.C.
so why should it matter if they get 2
letters or 500 letters opposing it?
Saving America depends of the
United States shedding all of these
foreign alliances that are entangling
the U.S. in the mis-adventures of its
allies. The United States is the
world's largest producer of crude oil.
Why then is it politically dependent
on Saudi Arabia? The United States
is 72 percent White and Christian, so
why has it entangled itself in the
domestic and foreign policies of the

SAVING AMERICA

Jewish state of Israel? Jews make up a very small percentage of the United States yet exert the most influence in American entertainment, banking, politics, and technology. Was this by chance or by design? Israeli Lobbyists spend millions of dollars a year through AIPAC meeting with American Congresspersons to influence them to continue giving 30 Billion Dollars a year to Israel, to vote on behalf of Israel, and to vote against legislation like BDS that could hurt Israeli goods.

Out of Touch Celebrities
Celebrities, whether in music, fashion, or movies, are symbols of popular culture that influence

SAVING AMERICA

society. Artists always want to look
like they are pushing the edge and at
the forefront of innovation. Now the
so-called "artists" in Hollywood act
like they are representative of
American values and representative
of American life. Since only 1
percent of the Humans on earth are
rich, it is safe to say that Celebrities
are out of touch with the struggles of
the working class and middle class.
The Liberals for too long acted as if
only minorities were facing economic
and financial problems and that all
Whites were rich. A falsity that was
pushed as a narrative by the
mainstream media and even
politicians like Bernie Sanders.
Celebrities are very rich and may at
one point been in tune with the

SAVING AMERICA

struggles of the average person, but forgot about it when they became rich. Still, despite being out of touch with the realities of America, they feel the need to bash Conservative ideals and Americana as being evil. Whether it is a music video promoting abhorrent behavior, lustful behavior, abortion, or other touchy subjects, the celebrities are attempting to pull apart the social fabric of society by subverting it and defacing it. Maybe the video producer is pushing that theme but the artist doesn't have to agree on it. The out of touch Hollywood celebrities believe that there fame and expertise in one field, acting, music, etc extends in to other fields like Political Consulting and Political

SAVING AMERICA

Advisory. That would be like a
person who is a Doctor believing that
they could perform an Engine
Transplant in a 1972 Chevy because
they have Medical Expertise.
Expertise and Accolades in one field
do not transfer in to another. The
political advice and political opinions
of Celebrities is un-wanted and
irrelevant. Nothing a celebrity has to
say in regards to politics has any
worth whatsoever. Hillary Clinton
had many pep rallies with celebrity
rappers, actors, actresses, and
musicians rooting for her. None of
that made any difference in the 2016
election because the out of touch
celebrities were part of the elite and
the vote for Trump in 2016 was
ironically a vote against the elite of

the nation. Hollywood and the White House had a chummy relationship under President Obama and rappers like Jay-Z were frequent guests at the White House. Obama used Jay-Z on several occasions to get his message out to the youth.

Musicians, Rappers, and Actors cheering for the President of the United States is one thing, but going out and giving their political opinions to the public as if they mattered is another. They are loved for what they do; making music, acting, dancing, etc. They are loved for playing imaginary characters. Some of the actors are stuck in a sort of time warp where they are unable to distinguish fantasy and reality causing them to continue playing the

role despite being outside the stage.
Actors have a right to a political
opinion but they should understand
that their opinion is just that, an
opinion. Their opinion holds no more
weight than the opinion of anyone
else. They know that by using their
face and acting fame to sell a
political message it will get people to
flock to them because of their fame,
so they do it. Every awards show
has turned in to an Anti-Conservative
platform with musicians and actors
trying to outdo each other in who can
grandstand harder and longer. The
awards shows have become a farce,
a parody like version of themselves.
The celebrities have used the bully
pulpit to spread messages that have
lead to social degeneracy in

SAVING AMERICA

American communities.
Conservatism is lampooned,
liberalism is celebrated, and anyone
that disagrees with this is either
branded a racist, sexist, or
xenophobe. Conservative actors,
conservative musicians, and
conservative celebrities are for the
most part shunned and branded as
Anti-Semitic. Gary Oldman and Mel
Gibson are two such actors that
have been outspoken regarding the
obvious and open Jewish control of
Hollywood but have been shunned
by the Hollywood Elite as being Anti-
Semitic. Liberalism and Socialism
are allied forces among Hollywood
celebrities and anyone that fails to
conform to these standards among
them faces being shunned, being

SAVING AMERICA

avoided, or being secretly or openly banned from the industry. The name of the game is "Get With The Program" or get left behind and shunned. Hollywood acts like the forefront of American thought and culture when in fact the 2016 Presidential Vote for Trump showed that the majority of Americans view Hollywood as a hotbed of social degeneracy and virtue signaling. Liberals in Hollywood for many years courted and honored sexual predators like Harvey Weinstein and Jeffrey Epstein, incidentally both of them Jewish and both of them were highly famous and influential. The Liberals in Hollywood said nothing of Weinstein and pretended like there were no "organized sex rings" in

SAVING AMERICA

Hollywood. The out of touch Hollywood celebrities were all behind Hillary Clinton in 2016. If these Hollywood Celebrities like George Clooney are so popular, famous, and well liked, then why weren't they listened to by the majority of Americans in 2016? The truth is that the Hollywood Elitists are viewed as just that, the Elite. They are viewed as the Elite by the majority of Americans and they are viewed as the Elite by the majority of the world. How many people own 30 Million Dollar Homes? The Elite own 30 Million Dollar Homes. The entertainment elite like actors and musicians are out of touch because their lives are anything but normal. They may do some normal things

SAVING AMERICA

like the rest of us but they are for the
most part detached and isolated
from the realities of day to day life for
Americans. Driving down trendy
Sunset Boulevard and eating $200
lunch at an outdoor trendy café is not
normal life for humans. The majority
of Americans live paycheck to
paycheck, that is how normal
Americans live. The elite,
entertainment or political or other, do
not lead normal lives that resemble
the lives of normal everyday
Americans. The elite live in an
almost fantasy like life and they
believe that everything can be
bought, changed, moved, twisted,
altered, or re-arranged to suit their
tastes.

SAVING AMERICA

Censorship of Conservatives

There has been an alarming trend among Tech Companies in the United States since 2016 and that has been the purposeful banning or censorship of Conservatives. Alex Jones was banned and censored on various social networks including Facebook and YouTube because he was blamed for being responsible for the election of Donald Trump to the United States Presidency in 2016. Donald Trump won because people were tired of the 8 years of Obama and wanted real change, which is something they were promised to by Obama but never received. Hillary Clinton also had left a bad taste with potential voters over things like missing emails. Clinton had little

SAVING AMERICA

likeability and Trump had the ability
and charisma to work the crowd.
Trump is an entertainer as well as a
successful businessman and he
used all the things he picked up in
entertainment to make even his
opponents laugh. Trump knew how
to win over an audience and Clinton
was depending on name recognition
and backdoor dealings to see it
through. Conservative media was
blamed for Hillary losing as well were
the Russians. Then certain members
of the Conservative Media were
blamed for being Russian operatives
acting on behalf of Russia to spread
Fake News. The Mainstream Media
has a horrible record when it comes
to spreading Fake News so it was
ironic for Liberals to start calling

SAVING AMERICA

Conservative Media fake news after Trump defeated Clinton. Twitter accounts of Conservative media members were shut down, YouTube channels were de-monetized, and Facebook Pages were shut down for spreading Conservative ideology. The tech companies, run by Billionaires, had chosen Hillary to win and Trump's victory was a slap in the face to the Liberal owned Silicon Valley companies in San Francisco and San Jose. They had to take action and they did. They shut down Conservative Media voices and Conservative outlets that they believed were important and instrumental in the election of Trump to the Presidency of the United States. The growth of Censorship in

SAVING AMERICA

the United States is as alarming as it is dangerous to the freedom of expression.

Fix Healthcare

The government should not be partnering with drug companies and health care providers. The government should not interfere in healthcare whatsoever and healthcare should be offered by licensed private companies. The free market will determine the price of healthcare and the free market will allow for competition which will in turn lower the prices of medical service. Doctors frequently prescribe 8 different types of pills to the same patient because the Doctor is billing the government for it. When healthcare is completely privatized, this will allow for new healthcare start-ups to find new and innovative ways to lower costs. Let the free market decide the cost of healthcare. Have you ever been to a government-run hospital? 2 hours or more in a seat waiting for sub-standard service. A completely private healthcare system would make companies have to compete further and further for your business which would result in you saving money. Price elasticity is a major factor in things like insurance, medical coverage, etc. People would flock overnight to the healthcare provider that provided the best service with the lowest price. That is how the Free Market works. When the market dictates prices the market is forced to innovate and lower them in order to keep their doors open. If they are not able to lower their prices they become bankrupt. Many budget service providers have been able to thrive in industries like air travel so why would the same idea not apply to healthcare? Saving America depends on completely privatizing healthcare services.

My President is American

During the 8 years of President Barack Hussein Obama in the U.S. Presidency, social media posts were frequently made saying things like "My President is Black". No one in the United States really questioned what this meant and why it was relevant. It showed that some Black people have a preference for Black people. That is all that it showed. When White male Donald Trump became President of the United States you may have heard people making posts like "My President is White", which showed that some White people have a preference for Whites. Was it racist for Obama supporters to say "My President is Black"? Is it racist for Trump supporters to say "My President is White"? Regardless of the amount of melanin in the skin of the U.S. President, your President is American. There are some Liberals that say "Not My President" which is even more laughable. If you are an American then whoever is elected as

SAVING AMERICA

the President of the United States is
your President whether you like them
or not. It is not up for debate
because whoever has been elected
was elected in a legal manner.

Feminism Gone Wild

Liberal Women in the United States
believe things like "Women are the
Future" and they say it often in social
media posts. What exactly does that
mean? Does that mean the future is
one in which men do not exist?
Liberal media buff Michael Moore
mentioned that "a step ladder" can
replace men jokingly. Why does the
Left believe with any sense of truth
that the future contains no men or
that men could be replaced? It is
acceptable for women to be paid as

much as men. That is not the issue of contention. The issue is that women openly belittle men and attempt to shame things like masculinity. The feminization of men is in full swing with movies, music, and popular culture media lampooning and ridiculing masculinity. What has the result been? The result has been that Marriage rates and Birth rates are at their lowest since after World War 2. A large portion of millennials vow to never get married at all because the tradition family model has been eroded by popular culture. Red (Republican) states still have higher marriage and birth rates than Blue (Democrat) states, but the fact still stands that marriage and birth rates are at their lowest they have been in 70 years. Men are openly discouraged against marriage and women are left behind looking for a man to step up and play the role of the Family Man. Some Single Mothers have been forced out of necessity to turn to despicable things like online prostitution and other immoral acts. The social consequences of lowered marriage and birth rates are permanent and real. Single Women and Single Men are thrown in to a sort of competition where they have to compete for the same resources. This makes Men and Women adversaries of each other instead of allies to each other. They aim to out-do one another in the hopes of getting the same position, and this makes them competitive, mean, cruel, and insensitive towards each other. Feminism has made Women insensitive and has made Men run from the Marriage altar. It is has resulted in the lowest marriage and birth rates since after WW2. Each Family is like a company that makes purchases and hire employees. A Family is a financially strong unit because more than one individual is able to contribute to its financial independence. As a financially independent unit, the family makes decisions that impact all of its family members. The Woman is in competition with a Man and the Man is in competition with a Woman, which means they are only thinking

SAVING AMERICA

about defeating each other and
winning at all costs. This has
hardened Women and made them
like Men while it has had the effect of
making Men like Women. It has
feminized men and made women in
to angry persons who "hate men"
and want a future without them. The
future is both men and women and
only one gender doesn't make a
family. A Family implies that there is
a Man and Woman in the equation.
Single Mothers are told by the
mainstream media to be angry and
act angry, as if anger will make
single men want to talk to you and
marry you. Many of the Women that
say that they want no man in the
house truly believe that and the
reason is that they are receiving

assistance from the government for their children. They have become dependent on the government to feed them and clothe them, therefore a man in the house would be un-necessary and un-warranted, in their opinion. It is important to understand that everything a Woman has in her life has been for the most part been provided to her by a Man, whether it be her Father, Boyfriend, Husband, or other. That is not to say that there aren't many Female entrepreneurs, because there are. Billionaires like Martha Stewart and Oprah are in fact Women that lead huge businesses. Whether they are Liberal or Conservative, they are Women that lead Billion Dollar businesses. But it is safe to say that for the most part, everything a Woman has did come from a Man who gave it to her, whether by inheritance or as a present. The feminization of men has made women angry because they see that men are not willing to get married, have children, and accept the responsibility of a family because the traditional family model has been eroded by society. The traditional family model is made fun of and lampooned openly on major media. Women are openly taught that they don't need a man. A family without a man in the house is not a family. A family is not Mother and Child. A Family includes the Father, which is something that is oblivious to the Liberal Left. 70 percent of the inhabitants of cities like Los Angeles are single and a large percentage of them will never get married in their life. They denied themselves this important Rite of Passage because mainstream popular culture and mainstream society taught them (social engineering) that it is okay to do so. The feminization of men and the hardening of women is a long term plan by the liberal elite to wipe out the traditional family model. The traditional family model that has worked for thousands of years is thought of as evil and outdated. The traditional family model which created billions of humans on this earth has been thrown away in favor of innovative schemes like Single Parent Family. The traditional family model exists not only for financial

SAVING AMERICA

reasons or for reasons of convenience, but also as a psychological support mechanism for each of the Family members. It has worked for thousands of years and has proven itself successful during that time. Women want to take it apart but it will only result in denying themselves opportunities like marriage and child birth, two rites of passage that provide us psychological satisfaction. From the 1980's, latch key kids became the norm and it would be normal for children to come home from school to find both parents gone. The television set became the parent and the mainstream media and popular culture became the teacher. Society changed because time was little and

SAVING AMERICA

responsibilities of employment had become mandatory for both parents. When the traditional family began to crumble, Single Parent Families became a regular occurrence and the amount of children with only one parent vastly increased. Divorce rates shot up to 50 percent and it was not un-common to see one or two parents going through several divorces in their lives. The slow destruction of the traditional family model meant that a new model had was slowly emerging. Where it has not or never been acceptable for Men to publicly trash Women, it suddenly became acceptable for Women to attack the very nature of Men. The first way that Women tried to attack Men is by claiming there are more than two genders. There are only two genders. You are biologically either a Man or a Woman. There is no 3rd option because it does not factually exist. Your genitals spell out your Gender and this is un-changeable except under the scalpel of a paid surgeon. Even if a Man where to get a Sex Change and become what is believed to be a Woman, the Man that has become a Woman would not be able to re-produce therefore they would still be a Man. Some Social Media platforms provide up to 52 different options for Gender when signing up to create a Profile. 52 different options? Why not 150 options or better yet 1000? (Being sarcastic!). There are only two options when it comes to the human race, you are biologically either a man or a woman. You can give 10000 options and call yourself a dolphin, but that does not change the reality of your Gender. Even a surgeon cannot change your Gender, all that a surgeon can do is mutilate and shape your body to look like a certain Gender. The imaginative creation of more than 2 Genders by Liberal Women has been a ruse that has been used to erode the traditional family model. If the Traditional Family model was totally flawed and in need of destruction, why has it worked so successfully for thousands of years? Look at yourself and your own parents and grandparents. If they never pro-created then you would not be reading this right now. The traditional family model is the only one that has proven itself to work despite what the Liberal establishment keeps promoting. Gay and Lesbian marriage has also strongly hurt the traditional family model. The celebrities, movie stars, musicians, and even mainstream media has packaged it and sold it to the public. They (celebrities, movie stars, musicians, and mainstream media) believe that by attaching themselves to this issue they are making themselves out to be important social justice warriors who are fighting for a good cause. It is virtue signaling meant to generate social media buzz and free publicity.

SAVING AMERICA

No one is born Gay or Lesbian or Transsexual. It is a behavior that has been promoted by popular culture and pushed to the youth. It is a behavior that is pushed on to society as being mainstream and normal when in fact only a small percentage of individuals in the United States are actually Gay, Lesbian, or Transsexual. It is in the fringe while the mainstream media promotes it as being mainstream. Nothing could be further from the truth. Women still want to get married to a Man and a Man still wants to get married to a Woman. Men and women want to have children and they want to build families. This is what it has always been and this is what it will always be. The Liberal Social Justice

SAVING AMERICA

Warriors in the United States can't change thousands of years of biology because a few celebrities promoted fringe behavior as mainstream. The Gay, Lesbian, and Transsexual movement has been a deliberate paid-for movement that is guided by individuals with an agenda. Their agenda, whether deliberate or not, has been the erosion of the Traditional Family model. It may be not clear who is paying for their agenda but it is clear that the agenda is to erode and if possible destroy the Traditional Family model and replace it with a new one.

SAVING AMERICA

Ban All Abortions

Ancient cultures practiced infanticide or the murdering of babies. The Canaanites practiced idolatry and worshipped a statue known as Moloch. Moloch was the patron deity of child sacrifice, also known as abortion. In a highly ritualistic ceremony, a baby would be placed between the arms of the Moloch statue and the arms were placed in such a way that the baby would slowly slip through the arms of the statue in to an open fire kiln below it. If the United States is so advanced, why then is it practicing infanticide or child murder? A baby is a human being that has the right to life and the right to be protected while still in the womb. A woman has the right to choose what to do with her body but she does not have the right to choose what she does with another human's body. A baby inside the womb of a mother is a living breathing human being, no matter what age it is. It has rights like any other human on earth. They have the right to be protected, whether as an infant or young child. Women see a potential ban on abortion as being wrong because it would potentially deny them the right to do that. To do what? To murder a baby? To murder an un-born child in the womb of the mother? Planned Parenthood has been at the forefront of abortions in the United States and there have been over 55 million abortions in the United States since its practice began. The Government should not be providing money to abortion clinics to kill babies. The Government should not be providing support to groups that carry out abortion. Women have the right to choose contraceptives before sex but women should not have the right to kill a barely grown human being in their womb, Women want the right to choose but the un-born have the right to life. If they were created in the womb they are a human being that will grow up to have the same aspirations, dreams, and wants as anybody else will. They have the right to life and they have the right to be protected within the womb of the mother. Murder is murder. Period.

SAVING AMERICA

Russian Hacking Hoax

After the 2016 Presidential election in which Donald Trump won, many on the Left created innuendo and false rumors regarding the hacking of the U.S. Presidential election by Russia. It was a lie perpetrated to de-legitimize the win by Trump and to push for a re-emergence of Cold War style foreign policy. It was embarrassing to Russia to be blamed for interfering in an election without there being proof provided, yet the Mainstream Media continued with this false narrative. If the Democratic Party was hacked, then they should protect their computers. The Democratic Party do not control elections and the Democratic Party is not the United States of America.

SAVING AMERICA

The 320 Million Americans in the
United States are the United States
of America. The Democratic Party is
an incorporation like a business
therefore it should protect its
systems better and take computer
privacy more seriously. The DNC is
not the Government of the United
States of America and it can act as if
it is a branch of the government. The
DNC is a political party with very
advanced computer security and
high tech software on its servers.
There is no proof whatsoever that
Russians hacked any State's
electoral systems. The mainstream
media spent nearly 2 and a half
years perpetuating what they knew
to be a lie. If there had been any
proof that Russians had meddled or

SAVING AMERICA

interfered in the 2016 U.S. Presidential election then it would have been presented to the public. The public were never shown any piece of evidence that could, without a doubt, tie Russia to meddling or interference in the 2016 U.S. Presidential election.

Right To Privacy

The right to privacy is a huge issue for Conservatives and they believe that it has been eroded by technologies used to control us including video surveillance, facial recognition, listening to our phone calls and phone conversations, and electronic surveillance that is conducted on our social media profiles and posts. If Freedom of

SAVING AMERICA

Speech is an American right, then
why are Americans being spied on?
The militarization of Police via the
Federal Government has provided
advanced military grade equipment
to local law enforcement officials,
giving them the means to listen to
your phone calls and screen your
information for collection. What if you
made a post that was subversive or
not in line with popular opinion?
Then you can be flagged as a
potential danger or put on a list of
individuals to be watched and
monitored. You could be put on a
watch list because your written
thoughts are deemed subversive.
The Thought Police hard at work.
The right to privacy means being
free from being watched, being free

SAVING AMERICA

from being listened to, being free from being monitored, and being free from control. Modern America has seen the right to privacy eroded for reasons of safety. To paraphrase Benjamin Franklin "If you are willing to trade your liberty for security, then you deserve neither". The right to privacy has been eroded because the good guys want to catch the bad guys. That means you have to be watched. The question is who will watch the watchers? Who will provide oversight so that the people watching you do not violate your rights? The idea of someone watching you (spying on you) or listening to you (eavesdropping) is not only frightening, it is also illegal. The erosion of privacy rights and the

SAVING AMERICA

disregard of many law enforcement individuals for your privacy rights, has revealed an alarming trend in American political life. The loss of Privacy Rights is a slippery slope that can lead to the further loss of rights. It is a dangerous precedent to set and it sends the message that the U.S. Constitution can be bypassed or avoided whenever it is politically feasible to do so. It sends the message that the rights which the Founding Fathers fought so hard for can be discarded and thrown in the waste basket like a piece of wet tissue. Rights are inalienable, granted by the U.S. Constitution and therefore cannot be taken away, but many people have illegally tried to deny them to others. Privacy rights, as other rights, were made to protect the rights of Americans from authoritarianism and an all-powerful central government. If privacy rights are eroded and not taken seriously, there is no reason to believe that the same won't happen to other rights. The loss of rights are a slippery slope that could easily lead to the loss of further rights in other areas. Saving America also means saving America from creeping Authoritarianism in the form of the loss of privacy rights.

Education

Public schools are not the best place to educate your children. Children that do not live in the area are bussed in to your child's school. You should have the right to choose where to school your children, not the government. The same amount that the government gives to a public school per student is also the same amount the government gives to a private school per student. When you enter a private school you can feel the difference in the quality between a private and public school. The bathrooms are cleaner, the students are nicer, the teachers are more attentive, and the place smells clean. Public schools, in many cases are a nightmare. Gang fights, random violence, horribly dirty bathrooms, aggravated teachers, and the students are a bit wilder (than private schools). Vouchers can be provided to parents so that they

SAVING AMERICA

can send their children private
charter schools that provide a higher
level of education in a generally
better environment. Public schools
and Private Charter schools should
exist and the Parents should be able
to choose where to send their
children, whether it be a public
school or private charter school. The
government is spending the same
amount per student with the
difference being that the Parents will
have the choice where to send their
children. Saving America depends
on you having the choice, rather than
the government choosing for you.
Some parents choose to send their
children to private institutions
because they believe that the
academic environment is more

stimulating and enriching. It should be a personal choice that the government should not interfere in. The parents can choose, if they want to, to send their children to a public school, but that too should be a personal choice.

Energy Self Sufficiency

The United States should take an isolationist approach towards achieving energy self-sufficiency. Self-sufficiency means breaking off alliances with nations in and around the Persian Gulf and focusing on being able to produce more than we consume on a daily basis. The United States is already the world's largest oil producer. Energy exploration should be incentivized

SAVING AMERICA

and energy companies (small or big) should be pushed towards increasing output. Crude Oil Petroleum may run out in less than 100 years but the United States and the rest of the world will have Natural Gas for at least 200 more years. By that time enough technologies will have been invented that can again give the lead to the United States in the energy sector. Oil companies are lambasted and ridiculed by the Left as being extinct and not useful anymore. The simple fact remains that wind and solar cannot provide the energy needs of the United States population. New exploration has to be encouraged and rewarded, so that new sources of oil and gas can be explored and brought to

SAVING AMERICA

production. A United States Naval Aircraft Carrier uses an entire Barrel of oil (approximately 75 gallons) every 3 feet that it travels. The United States is a heavy user of oil and gas and thus should re-invest in these industries in order to maintain its energy dominance.

Energy self-sufficiency strategy will depend on not only new exploration and re-investment, but will also depend on breaking any political foreign alliances that provide the United States with oil and gas. Political alliances tied to oil and gas hinder the independence of the United States by making America hostage to the whims and decisions of the allied nation. The political alliance with Saudi Arabia has been

SAVING AMERICA

a marriage of convenience, created simply for the matter of meeting the energy needs of the United States. Over 100 American oil companies have declared bankruptcy in the past few years due to cheap Saudi oil being dumped on the United States market making domestic oil companies unable to compete. The oil and gas sector in the United States is in need of protectionist policies that will stop cheap Saudi oil from being dumped on the American market because its consequences are bankruptcy and insolvency.

Social Engineered Society

What is a Social Engineered Society? It is a society in which the norms, taboos, and cultural nuances are directed by a group or a governing body. The term itself is Orwellian by nature and connotes a centrally controlled society that follows the wishes and precepts of its creator. Conservatives are told what words they can or can't use by popular culture. They are told what words are taboo, what words are now offensive, and what words are deemed important enough to be included in the English language. Going outside these norms can lead to being called a Racist or even a Conspiracy Theorist. What is a Conspiracy Theorist? A Conspiracy Theorist is a person that provides an alternative explanation for the same event or occurrence. The term was created to negatively portray anyone

SAVING AMERICA

that provided an alternative
explanation to an event or
occurrence. If you went outside
Conventional Wisdom you were
labeled a Conspiracy Theorist, in
order to show you as being mentally
unstable therefore unable to be
reasonable. In a socially engineered
society, you conform to the
conventional wisdom of the elites or
you are outcast as a conspiracy
theorist that probably needs a
psychologist. That is the Fascism of
the Left at work. Conform or else you
are a Racist or a Conspiracy
Theorist. Television shows, movies,
music, and popular culture are
socially engineered. Look at the Ken
doll of the Barbie toy brand. Ken was
a very masculine toy in the 1980's.

SAVING AMERICA

Over time the Ken doll was feminized and changed. A sign of the times but definitely telling about the direction popular culture was heading in. Popular culture was heading towards the feminization of Men and it happened as a slow and gradual process that happened over many years. A socially engineered society stifles innovation and encourages conformity. Any divergence outside of these norms is considered taboo and dangerous to society. A perfect example of a socially engineered environment are colleges and universities across the United States. Professors are for the most Liberal and teach their brand of conventional wisdom to their students. Any divergence outside of

SAVING AMERICA

the conventional wisdom as laid out
by the educational elite is considered
a threat to the intellectual
establishment. In the perfect socially
engineered environments of
universities and colleges, students
are trained in how to speak, what is
proper to say, and what goes outside
the norms of societal acceptance.
Liberals want to control your
language and they want the
government to police what language
you should or shouldn't use. They
have no concern with Freedom of
Speech. Their concern is with
shutting down speech that they
deem to be offensive to them and to
their cause. They act as if the
Freedom of Speech is only
applicable to things that they like and

SAVING AMERICA

does not apply to issues they disagree with. The attempt to shut down Free Speech en masse among Liberals has been a sign of their contempt for the ruling law of the land, the United States Constitution. If the Liberals loved America so much then they would defend your right to say what you pleased, even more so if they disagreed with it. Not having a popular opinion should not make you a villain or an outcast. Liberals, who incidentally live most along both coasts of the United States, feel that their view is the only correct one and every other voice should be shut down that does not follow the "norm" as has been laid out by them. Conservative speakers at protested at universities and colleges nationwide. Many Conservative speakers have had to cancel their speaking engagement out of fear of harm. Shutting down free speech is the new tactic of the Left. It is really an old Socialist tactic but it is one that will fail.

Participation as Obligation

In the United States, the role of the American citizen is to participate in the processes that keep America running. Civic responsibilities do not start or end at jury duty. Americans can take part in the political process in various ways and they include the following:

- Voting
- Joining a political party
- Helping with a political campaign

SAVING AMERICA

- Joining a civic group
- Joining a community group
- Giving an elected official your opinion on an issue
- Calling Senators and Representatives
- Publicly supporting or opposing an issue or policy
- Running for political office
- Writing an opinion editorial piece to a newspaper

Political participation makes the system work. All Americans want good government but they have to participate in the processes of government in order to have it. In other words, the government doesn't work unless you participate.

SAVING AMERICA

MOSTOFIZADEH'S HIERARCHY OF POLITICS

Whether it is through holding politicians accountable by voting them out of office or by direct involvement as a candidate, you have to participate if you want to see results that are beneficial to you. Taking the attitude of apathy and non-involvement puts you in isolation and prevents you from having any effect whatsoever on the political landscape. A Politician does not see an issue as being important unless

their constituents do. If you do not
care neither does the politician. Part
of political participation is to identify
and maintain communication with
elected officials that directly impact
your life, whether the City Council,
Congressional Representative,
Assemblyperson, or Dog Catcher. If
you do not maintain communication
with your elected officials then how
can you expect for them to listen to
you. You can directly Lobby an
elected official by contacting their
office and asking for an appointment
to meet with them. You can mail your
local representative and maintain
correspondence with them.
Politicians have an agenda and if
you seek the issue that concerns you
to be on their agenda then you have

SAVING AMERICA

to Lobby your elected official to take a stance on that issue. Only by communicating and interacting with your local official can you discover the stance that politician has taken or you may discover that they have taken no position at all allowing you to present the issue at hand. Being an American is about participating in the processes of government by interacting with your local officials. Certain politicians like Congressional Representatives are legally obligated to register your mail and cannot deny your correspondence as publicly elected servants of the people. It is your responsibility to make the effort to contact local elected officials and to communicate your views to them. The American citizen's role in the

SAVING AMERICA

American republic is to participate so that publicly elected officials can be held accountable for what they say and how they vote. Public participation is not something to be taken lightly. If you want to hold your local official accountable, you should make it systematic and organized. Create a "Voting Report Card" to keep track of how your local, state, or federal official voted on various topics. Assign a Grade (A to F) for each issue and keep track of it so that you can discuss their voting record with them. One of the main ways to keep your representative accountable is by keeping a record of their voting record and this is why the importance of doing this cannot be understated.

SAVING AMERICA

No Safe Zones Needed

The idea that humans should be given safe zones where they can express themselves in the United States is wholly ludicrous and preposterous. The Freedom of Speech is the right of every American regardless of where they are. If you have to have a safe zone to speak in, then you are probably being denied the Constitutional right to express yourself. After the election of Trump to the US Presidency in 2016, people began to speak of so called safe zones and wearing safety pins to denote their acceptance of safe zones. It was more of a publicity stunt than anything else, but the mainstream media fawned over it and the celebrities that sold wearing it. Freedom of speech is not based on safe zones or safety pins. The Freedom of Speech extends everywhere and is applicable everywhere. Entertainment elites sold the idea of safe zones and safety pins so that they could earn points with Liberals by virtue signaling. If the Liberals were really concerned about preserving the speech of all Americans then Liberals wouldn't make such a concerted effort to shut down every type of speech that they disagreed with. It was good for creating temporary excitement but the idea of creating safe zones for free speech is as ridiculous as it is asinine. Free Speech is guaranteed to every American wherever they are. Free

SAVING AMERICA

Speech has limits of course, for example, it is illegal to falsely yell "Fire" in a crowded theater or to falsely yell "Bomb" on a crowded airplane. It is illegal to do so because of the panic that will ensue causing un-seen consequences like humans trampling each other to death and more. But other than that, you are free to express yourself freely. The entire United States is a free speech Safe Zone. The idea that a safe zone has to be created specifically for minorities, people of color, and certain religions is both demeaning and un-American. If the entire United States is a free speech Safe Zone, than there is no reason to create additional areas designated for speaking. All of America is either safe to speak in or else free speech is non-existent. Private tech corporations have de-platformed individuals they dislike but they cannot deny your right to free speech. Their Terms of Service could reject you but a Tech company as a whole is not able to deny you free speech. No one is able to deny anyone else Free Speech but Liberals do it consistently by attempting to shut down individuals that they disagree with. Anywhere you go on earth, people more or less respect and love the nation they live in. In America, you have people coming here that want to preach about how bad America is while taking advantage of its benefits. Does that make them bad people?

SAVING AMERICA

No. Dissent is the highest form of patriotism. If something is wrong or needs to be made better than it should be pointed out and the person that points it out should not be vilified because they do so. If we believe in Freedom of Speech then complaining about problems we see or face is a part of it. Remember that Freedom of Speech doesn't only apply to issues you like or agree with. It is most certainly true that America has a myriad of problems like any nation on earth but in America you are still free to speak your mind without fear of being arrested. If Alex Jones was in China for example, instead of having his social media accounts shut down, he might have been thrown in to a prison cell. Instead of having his social media accounts shut down, he might have been denied the right to travel. I understand why people are so happy to become Americans legally and to travel to America. Although the United States has a myriad of problems, it is still the greatest nation on earth. It needs fine tuning and it depends on the citizenry to hold each other and to hold public officials accountable. Patriotic feelings for America and should be encouraged and loved. Wearing a hat that says Make America Great Again is a symbol of pride for those that love America. There are various videos circulating on YouTube showing angry Liberals tearing off the aforementioned hat off

SAVING AMERICA

the heads of Conservatives. Totally unacceptable behavior by Liberals but it is encouraged and pushed by the Left. Why do Liberals think that it is acceptable behavior to steal another person's property because they don't agree with the message on it? Since when has that become acceptable behavior? Whether you are a Liberal or a Conservative or a Libertarian or Independent you should want to Make America Great Again. You should want to make wherever you live great again. If you hate where you live then move to a place that is more to your liking. There are many English that actually choose to live in Spain. There are many Polish that actually choose to live in England. There are many

SAVING AMERICA

people from Belgium that choose to live in Thailand. It is a personal decision that each person has to make in their own life. Just because you are born somewhere doesn't mean that you are confined to that area for the rest of your life. Humans travel and humans move to areas that they see more beneficial to them. There are 220 nations on earth and there are many advanced Western democracies in the Western hemisphere, ranging from Sweden to the Netherlands to Spain. People are not forced to live in the United States, they choose to. If they want to be an American then they should invest time in Americana and have love for its beginning and history. They should learn about the cultural intricacies of America so that they can better understand it. A feel of patriotism should be derived from loving what it stands for. Patriotism should not be derived from national tragedies or war. Patriotism should be derived from loving what the United States of America uniquely represents.

Lower All Taxes

The reason that the American colonists revolted against England was because of Taxation without Representation. The United States was born on the issue of taxes. Lowering taxes boosts businesses by allowing them to preserve money to be used for hiring new employees, buying equipment, and developing

SAVING AMERICA

new products and services. The lower the tax rate, the stronger the economy will operate. High taxes hurt the middle and working class more than they do the rich. The rich use tax havens and offshore banking to reduce their tax to nearly zero. The middle class and working class do not have access to Bahamian banks and offshore accounts. The middle class and working class depend on tax breaks to lower their expenses. The majority of businesses in the United States happen to be small businesses rather than large mega-corporations. Small businesses rely on tax breaks to grow their businesses. Higher taxes means less money for businesses to hire new employees and purchase new equipment. Higher taxes means less incentive to achieve greater levels of productivity, as well because whatever is produced and sold will be done so at a higher tax rate. The rich do not gain more from a lower tax rate than do the working or middle class. It can be stated, however, that the middle and working class stand to gain more from a lower tax rate than the rich. Everyone wins with a lower tax rate. America becomes more competitive because a lower tax rate provides a concrete financial incentive to corporations to incorporate in the United States. The rich use nations like Ireland, New Zealand, and other rich Tax Havens to store their wealth. If the United

SAVING AMERICA

States drops its tax rate lower than tax havens, then that would attract billions of dollars to the United States.

20 Trillion Dollar Debt

The United States has nearly 20 Trillion Dollars in debt. This means that every American owes practically $40,000 to nations that hold America's debt. Government shutdowns, bank holidays, and employees asked to work without pay are slowly becoming the norm in Washington DC. The United States has to keep borrowing and selling its debt to nations like China and Japan in order to maintain its high expenditure. Debt makes nations captive to the debtors, who end up influencing political and fiscal policy in the debtor nation. Because much of the debt of the United States is packaged and sold to foreign nations, it makes the United States vulnerable to foreign influence and even foreign control. Debt weakens an economy by weakening the value of its currency. Worst of all, debt makes a nation susceptible to the political intrigues of those nations in to which it is indebted. The nations that hold the debt of the United States could decide to better their chances of getting paid back by attempting to influence the outcome of a political election or by lobbying politicians to work against the interests of Americans. The loyalty of the nations that control America's debt are to themselves and not to America. Self-interest, greed, and profit are their concerns, not Americans. Debt cripples the economy and puts a huge strain on business. All debt is not evil, it is the debt that is un-manageable that negatively affects the economy. Debt for an important jobs project that could help the economy through job creation is not necessarily bad. Debt for building a bridge that could boost trade between two cities is not bad debt. Trillions of Dollars in Debt generated through military adventurism is bad debt. Hundreds of Billions of Dollars wasted on weapons that will never be used is bad debt. Hundreds of Billions of Dollars wasted on Afghanistan, Iraq,

SAVING AMERICA

Syria, and Libya is bad debt. Bailing out Wall Street Bankers is bad debt. Debt created for the construction of a nationwide high speed rail network is good debt. It is debt that can be paid back by passengers via use of the high speed rail network. It is important to understand the difference between good and manageable debt and bad debt generated through wasteful ventures. It is not a matter of debt being bad by itself. It is a matter of debt that is wasted by being used on fruitless ventures. The United States and all nations on earth generate debt, but the difference is in how the debt is used. Good debt is debt that is manageable and can be paid back. Debt generated for the

SAVING AMERICA

construction of an airport or sea port is good debt as it is manageable because it can be paid back by their use. Debt generated for the construction of a Toll Highway is good debt because it will generate money to pay back the debt. Bad debt is un-manageable and wasted. If America wants to steer the economy on the right course, it has to invest in job creation as well as in paying down the National Debt. 20 Trillion Dollars puts a strain on the ability of the government to operate. This causes the government to print more money causing wide-spread inflation. Prices are raised in some sectors causing other economic sectors to respond and raise their prices. For example, Rents are raised on property causing the local Bakery, the local Dry Cleaners, and the local Market to respond by raising prices on the goods they are selling. It is an economic chain reaction that results in prices being arbitrarily raised on goods and services. The growing 20 Trillion Dollar National Debt also sends shockwaves throughout the system allowing for events like recessions. As long as the United States is held hostage by foreign nations that control its debt, the United States must pay heed to the directions of the nations that hold America's debt. Liberals are afraid of nations like Russia hacking a U.S. election but care little about nations buying up America's debt with the aim of

SAVING AMERICA

leveraging it in to political influence to steer America's domestic affairs. The Left does not grasp the danger of having America's debt in the grips of foreign nations. An out of control national debt is not only dangerous for the economy but dangerous for the political future of the nation. National Debt opens up the U.S. to political intrigue therefore an ever growing National Debt is actually a National Security concern because its consequences extend in to the political sphere as well as the economic one. If you want to save America then the National Debt has to be paid off so the U.S. will return to a state of financial well-being. The burden created by the National Debt has far reaching consequences

SAVING AMERICA

which many not be identified or projected by economic experts. Sudden shifts in the economy due to the ever growing National Debt could de-stabilize the dollar and cause capital markets to go in a free-fall. If America wants to be more secure it should focus on the National Debt. Foreign wars, military adventurism, nation building, and empire management requires huge resources. Where does this money come from? Loans that increase the National Debt resulting in inflation and other un-seen economic consequences. War is Debt. The true value of a military conflict is in the debt that is generated. Whoever controls the debt usually controls the conflict. The United States has spent most of its history in various wars and each one added to the National Debt. Every in-coming administration has made a remark or two about paying down the National Debt without there being any real action taken. Debt can lead to financial disaster and economic recession.

Atheist Socialist Agenda

They go hand in hand and have been partners politically and socially. In the 20th century alone, nearly 200 million human beings were murdered by Atheistic Socialist Dictators like Mao in China, Stalin in Russia, Pol Pot in Cambodia, and Hitler in Germany. Hitler was most certainly a Socialist as well as a Nationalist. 200 Millions being killed because

SAVING AMERICA

Atheistic Socialist leaders wanted to erase religion from society and to create a new order that answered to them. To say Socialism kills would be valid but to say Socialism plus Atheism has killed many is even more valid. The move by Liberals to erase Prayer and to erase things like the Ten Commandments off of public buildings have shown the extent to which they will go to erase religion from society. The Founding Fathers were not heavily religious and some of them like Thomas Paine were irreligious to the point of apostasy, but they all understood the importance of morality in society. They all believed that each American should be free to worship as they wished but also recognized the importance of religious institutions and the social role they have in society. They wanted to keep it separate from politics without shunning it. It was a balancing act for the Founding Fathers as much as it for modern Americans. The Founding Fathers believed that God had given them Providence in the form of allowing a small rag-tag army of irregulars and militiamen to defeat England, who was at that time the powerful military nation on earth. They believed that God had played a role in their victory and that God was instrumental to their victory over England. The Founding Fathers wanted to keep religion separate from politics but didn't want religion and belief in God to be stripped from society. They believed that God was watching over and protecting America as had been displayed in the Revolutionary War. Liberals want to downplay the importance of the Founding Fathers and brush them off because of their having owned slaves. The slave trade has never been sanctioned or approved of by the government of the United States at any point in history. Slavery was an economic problem for the United States that had to be solved. It was not a matter of race, it was a matter of money. Slaves were essentially free labor for Southerners while Northerners had to compete with free labor. You cannot compete with free labor. It might have been good for a few plantation owners in the

SAVING AMERICA

South but it was not good for the nation because it forced Northerners to compete with the free labor of Southerners. It benefitted a very small few at the expense of the many. Lincoln did not originally want to go to war but he did not want the nation to split apart either. However evil we see Slavery as in modern times, it was an acceptable practice in many parts of the world even up to 50 years. You cannot judge 300 years ago with the lens of today. Slavery was an evil and it was eradicated because it was un-American. Liberals want to tear down the statues of important figures in American history because they believe the statues are racist symbols. The Founding Fathers

SAVING AMERICA

were not only not Racist, but they actively promoted brotherhood and love among Americans. For some modern Americans to claim that statues of key figures in American history should be torn down because we disagree with them would be doing a dishonor and disservice to the efforts the Founding Fathers made in the creation of America. Where does it stop? It starts with one statue and could lead to ten statues being torn down because some people disagree with them or dislike them. The Atheist Socialists in American society would love nothing better than to tear down the past of America and put up new statues in their place. Let me guess.....they would be statues of Socialist icons would they not? Attempting to tear up the past of America makes Liberals imply that they are the Future of America. It as if saying America was bad makes them good. The attempt by the Atheist Socialists and Liberals to tear away God from school has been a deliberate plan to say that the past on which America was made is not worthy of admiration. There are no Atheists in Foxholes is a true statement. The Founding Fathers believed without a doubt that God had intervened in their affairs and given them the strength and ability to defeat the powerful English Redcoats. The Founding Fathers believed Providence had delivered them from certain destruction at the hands of the well-equipped, well-armed, and highly trained Redcoat regulars. The Continental Army was anything but regular, in fact it was filled with irregulars that couldn't shoot straight. The irregulars would literally run and flee when they saw Redcoats. Anyone who believed that a rag-tag army of irregulars and conscripts would defeat the mighty English empire would have been laughed at and discounted. It is under these impossible conditions that men turn to God for help and the Founding Fathers were no exception. They also turned to God and asked for His assistance and they surely received it. The Founding Fathers would have probably looked at an Atheist as a deluded, misguided individual

SAVING AMERICA

seeking attention. None of the Founding Fathers were Atheists and even Thomas Paine, who was hardly religious, recognized the existence of God and His involvement in the affairs of Americans. Saving America depends on saving America from creeping Atheism that seeks to remove God from society. The Liberals have unsurprisingly been the beacon of Atheism and have actively attempted to re-shape the fabric of American society through the removal of Prayer from schools. America was established on the belief in God and built by God fearing men and women that believed that God's providence delivered them from the wrath of the mighty English empire. The English

SAVING AMERICA

army and the Continental Army had
chaplains that spoke to the injured
and dying as well as carried out
religious ceremonies. To say that
God was not incorporated in to the
creation of American culture would
be to deny the realities that took
place. Religion and morality played a
huge role in the development of
American life and the Church was
more often than not the center of the
community, an informal town-hall for
the exchange of words and ideas.
The misguided plan by Liberals to
erase Prayer and God from the
public sphere has revealed their
hatred for what America stands for.

SAVING AMERICA

United Nations

The United Nations was created to be a logical progression to the League of Nations. It was created in the United States to establish an international rule based order. The majority of the expenses of the United Nations are paid for by the United States. The United Nations doesn't make the world any safer and the United Nations' resolutions are not binding and enforceable. It is more or less, a speakers forum for diplomats to express the views of their respective nations to the press and public. The United Nations expense does not equal its benefit to the United States. The immense cost and responsibility of providing security, the immense costs in its administration, and the immense costs of its programs do not really benefit the United States. International diplomacy already exists between nations via consulates and embassies, attaches and diplomats, and between ambassadors of nations. The United Nations is an extra cost for the United States that could bind U.S. companies to its international resolutions resulting in the loss of revenue and insolvency. It is nice to have but not mandatory for diplomacy or for maintaining an international rule based order.

SAVING AMERICA

MIKAZUKI PUBLISHING HOUSE™
(U.S.P.T.O. Serial Number 85705702)

1) 25 Principles of Martial Arts
2) 25 Principles of Strategy
3) American Antifa
4) Arctic Black Gold
5) Art of War
6) Back to Gold
7) Basketball Team Play Design Book
8) Beginner's Magicians Manual
9) Boxing Coloring Book
10) California's Next Century 2.0
11) Camping Survival Handbook
12) Captain Bligh's Voyage
13) Coming to America Handbook
14) Customer Sales Organizer
15) DIY Comic Book
16) DIY Comic Book Part II
17) Economic Collapse Survival Manual
18) Find The Ideal Husband
19) Football Play Design Book
20) Freakshow Los Angeles
21) Game Creation Manual
22) George Washington's Farewell Address
23) Hagakure
24) History of Aliens
25) I Dream in Haiku
26) Internet Connected World
27) Irish Republican Army Manual of Guerrilla Warfare

SAVING AMERICA

28) Japan History Coloring Book
29) John Locke's 2nd Treatise on Civil Government
30) Karate 360
31) Learning Magic
32) Living the Pirate Code
33) Magic as Science and Religion
34) Magicians Coloring Book
35) Make Racists Afraid Again
36) Master Password Organizer Handbook
37) Mikazuki Jujitsu Manual
38) Mikazuki Political Science Manual
39) MMA Coloring Book
40) Mythology Coloring Book
41) Mythology Dictionary
42) Native Americana
43) Ninja Style
44) Ouija Board Enigma
45) Palloncino
46) Political Advertising Manual
47) Quotes Gone Wild
48) Rappers Rhyme Book
49) Saving America
50) Self-Examination Diary
51) Shinzen Karate
52) Shogun X the Last Immortal
53) Small Arms & Deep Pockets
54) Stories of a Street Performer
55) Storyboard Book
56) Swords & Sails

SAVING AMERICA

Facebook.com/MikazukiPublishingHouse

KAMBIZ MOSTOFIZADEH TITLES

SAVING AMERICA

Facebook.com/KambizMostofizadeh

If the Mikazuki Publishing House™ book is not available, place a request with any bookstore to order it for you.